MEN-AT-ARMS S...

EDITOR: MARTIN WINDROW

Napoleon's Hussars

Text by   EMIR BUKHARI

Colour plates by   ANGUS McBRIDE

OSPREY PUBLISHING LONDON

Published in 1978 by
Osprey Publishing Ltd
Member company of the George Philip Group
12—14 Long Acre, London WC2E 9LP
© Copyright 1978 Osprey Publishing Ltd

Reprinted 1981, 1982, 1983, 1984, 1985,
1987 (twice), 1988

ISBN 0 85045 246 5

Filmset by BAS Printers Limited,
Over Wallop, Hampshire
Printed in Hong Kong

The author would like to express his gratitude for the
assistance rendered him by the following persons in the
preparation of this book: the members of the staffs of
the Musée de l'Armée, Paris, and the National Army
Museum, London; Gerry Embleton; Jean de
Gerlache de Gomery; Richard Hook; Michel Risser;
Caroline Lederer; Maximilian da Luigi Luccese;
Chris Brennan. Finally and most importantly: M.
Lucien Rousselot whose researches and illustrations
since the first quarter of this century have rendered the
study of the *Grande Armée* of the first quarter of the
previous century possible in the style of this present series.

Organisation

Doubtless the most distinctive of all forms of light horse, the hussars originated in eastern Europe and, by means of their dress, their roots can be traced all the way back to a cavalry corps of the mighty Ottoman Empire: the Gunalis, whose rather eccentric fur-covered, tall conical caps and fur-lined jackets, perilously draped over the left shoulder, were to set a military fashion from Turkey to Hungary and thence, by way of Germany and France, to the rest of the world.

In contrast to their fellow light cavalry, the numerous regiments of indigenous French *chasseurs à cheval*, the hussars consisted of only fourteen regiments during the Empire. Six of these existed well before the massive reorganisations of 1791 and the rest were raised over the following years: the 7th and 8th regiments in 1792; the 9th, 10th and 11th in 1793; the 12th in 1794; the 13th in 1795; and, finally, the 14th in 1814.

These regiments were composed of four squadrons, themselves comprising two companies each of which in turn consisted of two troops or *peletons*. See *Napoleon's Dragoons and Lancers* and *Napoleon's Cuirassiers and Carabiniers* for the precise hierarchy of inter-regimental command, enumerating company and *état-major* NCOs and officers. In this title the role of light cavalry will be examined in the same manner in which we studied that of the heavy and medium.

Both the offensive and defensive roles of light cavalry consisted of reconnaissance on the one hand and advance, flank and/or rear and outpost protection of the main column on the other.

Although the hussars made their first real impact in 1806 with their astonishing pursuit of the Prussians over 1,160kms from the river Saale to the Oder in twenty-five days (capping this feat on arrival when, by dint of audacious demonstrations

by the 500 men of the combined 5th and 7th Hussars, the 6,000-strong Prussian garrison was bluffed into capitulating its fortress at Stettin along with 160 cannon), the large-scale use of flying

Colonel de Juniac of the 1st Hussars in full dress, 1807. This colonel's uniform provides us with a classic illustration of early officers' dress. His shako is basically the 1801 pattern but has variations which first appeared around 1802, such as a centrally placed cockade and loop; the headgear lacks both the detachable peak and the turban, which characterised the true 1801 model. The uniform is of note for its increasingly outdated cut and style: the dolman was to become sharper in cut, the pelisse less sack-like and considerably shorter, and the breeches were beginning to give way to trousers and overalls. (Van Huen. NAM)

Key to the figures on pp. 4 and 5:

A: *Adjutant* (adjutant)
AM: *Adjutant-major* (regimental-sergeant-major)
B: *Brigadier* (corporal)
Bf: *Brigadier-fourrier* (quarter-master corporal)
C: *Capitaine* (captain)
L: *Lieutenant* (lieutenant)
M: *Maréchal-des-logis* (sergeant)
Mc: *Maréchal-des-logis-chef* (sergeant-major)
Sl: *Sous-lieutenant* (second lieutenant)
T: *Trompette* (trumpeter)

A squadron of hussars in column by fours. Drawn up in this formation, a squadron would present a frontage of 4 metres and extend approximately 138 metres.* The column by fours, and even by twos when necessary, was most commonly reverted to when the squadron or regiment was obliged to keep to the roads; on a fair surface, the column would travel at around 6 or 7 kilometres an hour.

* All measurements are calculated exclusive of outriders.

A lead squadron of hussars in *colonne par divisions*. With the troops of each company now riding abreast, the squadron's frontage would expand to 24 metres and its depth would contract to 30 metres. Notice that the companies are drawn up in such a manner as to enable the rearmost to wheel to right or left without hindrance.

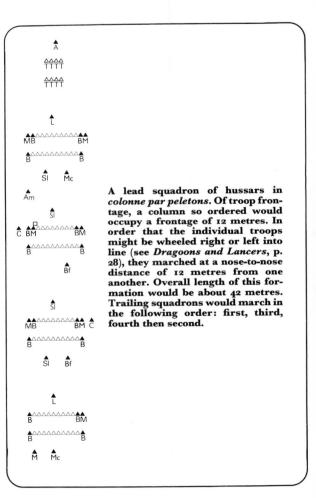

A lead squadron of hussars in *colonne par pelotons*. Of troop frontage, a column so ordered would occupy a frontage of 12 metres. In order that the individual troops might be wheeled right or left into line (see *Dragoons and Lancers*, p. 28), they marched at a nose-to-nose distance of 12 metres from one another. Overall length of this formation would be about 42 metres. Trailing squadrons would march in the following order: first, third, fourth then second.

columns of *blitzkrieg*-style cavalry was never developed. Imaginative employment of highly mobile spearheads was confined to patrols of between twenty and a hundred men and consequently when, in October 1806, twenty hussars led by a *sous-lieutenant* walked unopposed into Leipzig, the bulk of the *Grande Armée* was bogged down 80kms away at Jena, incapable of exploiting the opportunity.

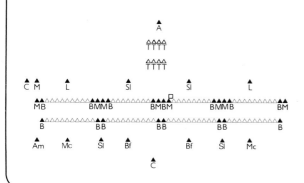

A lead squadron of hussars drawn up *en colonne serré*. In order to contract the depth of the column still further, squadrons would arrange their companies in this manner. The fully extended front would now measure some 48 metres, while the depth would shrink to a mere 6 metres. Following squadrons would probably not allow less than a troop's frontage to separate them from the squadron in front. In this way, a regiment in column might not exceed a depth of 54 metres (assuming a standard regiment of four squadrons).

Confined for the most part to scouring the countryside in the vicinity of the main columns, the hussar regiments would deploy their squadrons in battle order and sweep the surrounding landscape. Upon contact with the enemy, a troop of the leading squadron would disperse at the gallop to form a screen of sharpshooters about the regiment's front. If engaged, the hussar skirmishers would discharge their carbines at less than a hundred metres from a stationary position, their primary targets being enemy officers. Then, pistol in the right hand and drawn sabre hanging from the swordknot at the wrist, they would charge home, reserving the pistol ball to the last moment, then passing the handgun to their left hand and setting-to with cold steel.

Where such a charge required the back-up of the entire regiment, the squadrons would advance in extended waves staggered obliquely to either right or left, for maximum strike value.

Their defensive role might be described as the same as above but in reverse: maintaining surveillance of the enemy by forcing a contact, thereby eliminating any element of surprise, and masking the true movement of the main column by feints and general harassment.

This trouble-shooter role created a strong *esprit de corps* which resulted in the light cavalry believing itself to be rather more than just a cut above the rest. Indeed, such was the audacity of the hussars that their arrogant indiscipline brought a specific rebuke from the Emperor: 'These hussars must be made to remember that a French soldier must be a horseman, infantryman and artilleryman, and there is nothing he may turn his back on!'

Nowhere is evidence of their excesses, indulgences and pure egotism better illustrated than in their near-anarchic mode of dress.

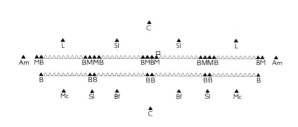

A squadron of hussars in battle order. In similar formation to the *colonne serré*, a squadron so ordered would find its regiment deployed alongside in either a straight line or in echelon, reading from right to left: first, second, third and finally fourth squadron. It should not be assumed, however, that formation of such a battle order was a prerequisite to combat; the precise manner in which a particular body of cavalry would enter the fray depended on its size and its preparedness—a regiment might, for instance, advance extended in echelon with its squadrons formed up in *colonne par pelotons* (i.e. troop frontage, see *Dragoons and Lancers*, p. 27).

Dress and Equipment

Hussar costume consisted principally of a short shell-jacket, the dolman; tight Hungarian riding breeches; calf-length Hungarian boots; and a second jacket slung on the left shoulder—the pelisse. Equipment comprised a shako, musketoon, curved sabre, sabretache, cartridge-pouch and attendant webbing. Accessories included short gloves, swordknot and barrel-sash. It is the enormous variety of these objects in their differing cuts, models and patterns that render hussar uniforms so complex; the following descriptions are therefore basic outlines, and readers are referred to the numerous black and white illustrations and their captions for further detail. This bewildering diversity of costumes represents just some of the costumes worn by just one regiment in the span of eleven years.

The hussar regiments were colourfully distinguished from one another by the different base cloths used in the manufacture of the dolmans, pelisses and breeches, and also by their facings and lace colours, as the chart below indicates.

Tunics

Unlike the pelisse, the dolman was fastened along its entire length by eighteen half-round buttons and their corresponding braid loops; in contrast, the pelisse loops were cut so that only the top five were long enough to be used. Both garments commonly had five rows of buttons except for those of the 2nd, 4th, 5th, 9th and 10th Hussars, which had only three rows. The pelisse was secured on the shoulder by a length of doubled-over cord which passed over the right shoulder and was then looped about a toggle sewn to the opposite side of the collar.

For other than full-dress occasions, hussars wore either the dolman or the pelisse beneath which they wore a sleeveless waistcoat. This garment was either single- or double-breasted and plain, or with miniature rows of buttons and braid identical to

Colonel Rouvillois of the 1st Hussars in full dress 1804–5. He wears an 1801-pattern shako, minus *flamme* but covered in scarlet cloth, with a centrally placed cockade and shako-plate; although this was increasingly the fashionable mode, it is interesting to note that his plume still reserves its old position on the right side of the headgear. The cords which loop about his left shoulder are just visible; their role was to become totally obsolete with the widespread introduction of chin-scales. His magnificent horse furniture is typical of that affected by superior officers, comprising metal-studded harness and leopard-skin schabraque liberally festooned with silver lace. (Benigni. Courtesy NAM)

Regt	Dolman	Collar	Cuffs	Pelisse	Breeches	Lace
1	Sky blue	Sky blue	Red	Sky blue	Sky blue	White/silver
2	Brown	Brown	Sky blue	Brown	Sky blue	White/silver
3	Silver grey	Silver grey	Red	Silver grey	Silver grey	Red/silver
4	Indigo	Indigo	Scarlet	Scarlet	Indigo	Yellow/gold
5	Sky blue	Sky blue	White	White	Sky blue	Yellow/gold
6	Scarlet	Scarlet	Scarlet	Indigo	Indigo	Yellow/gold
7	Dark green	Scarlet	Scarlet	Dark green	Scarlet	Yellow/gold
8	Dark green	Scarlet	Scarlet	Dark green	Scarlet	White/silver
9	Scarlet	Sky blue	Sky blue	Sky blue	Sky blue	Yellow/gold
10	Sky blue	Scarlet	Scarlet	Sky blue	Sky blue	White/silver
11	Indigo	Scarlet	Scarlet	Indigo	Indigo	Yellow/gold
12	Scarlet	Sky blue/scarlet	Scarlet/sky blue	Sky blue	Sky blue	White/silver
13	Brown	Sky blue	Sky blue	Brown	Sky blue	White/silver
14	Dark green	Scarlet	Scarlet	Dark green	Scarlet	White/silver

P. Benigni.

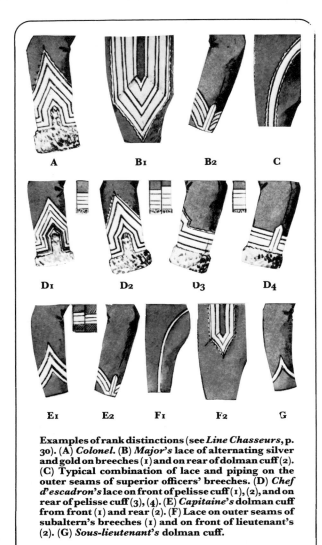

Examples of rank distinctions (see *Line Chasseurs*, p. 30). **(A)** *Colonel.* **(B)** *Major's* lace of alternating silver and gold on breeches (1) and on rear of dolman cuff (2). **(C)** Typical combination of lace and piping on the outer seams of superior officers' breeches. **(D)** *Chef d'escadron's* lace on front of pelisse cuff (1), (2), and on rear of pelisse cuff (3), (4). **(E)** *Capitaine's* dolman cuff from front (1) and rear (2). **(F)** Lace on outer seams of subaltern's breeches (1) and on front of lieutenant's (2). **(G)** *Sous-lieutenant's* dolman cuff.

those on the dolman. For fatigue-duty, a dark green single- or double-breasted linen stable-jacket was worn, occasionally equipped with shoulder-straps.

The 1812 Regulations prescribed the following changes: a slim braid shoulder-strap was to be sewn to the left shoulder of the dolman and pelisse to secure the webbing; the waistcoat, or *gilet*, was henceforth to be plain and single-breasted, fastening by means of ten cloth-covered buttons; and the stable-jacket was to be knitted and single-breasted with ten uniform buttons.

Rank distinctions were indicated by chevrons of lace above the cuffs, as shown in the illustration on this page. Further reference is available in *Napoleon's Line Chasseurs*, p. 30.

Legwear

Riding breeches were of the tight-fitting Hungarian pattern with lace ornamenting the outer seams and the edges of the front flap which disguised the button-up fly, where it took the form of Hungarian knots, simple trefoils or bastion-loops. From Republican times, however, it was found more practical to envelop them in overalls in order to save wear and tear.

Overalls were cut of blue, grey, green and even red material. They opened down the side by means of eighteen bone or pewter buttons along the outer seams. The inside leg and cuffs were reinforced with leather to varying degrees. For fatigues, they would be replaced by overalls of rough, unbleached cloth.

The 1812 Regulations specified that the ornamentation of the front flap of the breeches should consist of the simple bastion-loop. They also officially recognised the overalls and required them to be cut of dark green cloth with eighteen blackened bone buttons and leather cuffs rising to a height of 11cm. By this date, however, overalls had developed as a garment and we might more readily identify them nowadays as trousers; they were equipped with a front fly concealed by a flap, but frequently still bore lace or piping and/or buttons the length of the outer seams. Some examples have buttons at the calf to facilitate their use over the high riding boots, others have the leather cuff extended to the height of the boots and the top scalloped in imitation of them.

Capes and greatcoats

Hussars were issued a cape with hood of immense proportions dating back to the Monarchy; re-

Trooper and brigadier in drill uniform, 1807–10. These figures afford us a good look at the *bonnet de police* fatigue-cap common to all troops of the *Grande Armée*; although here smartly tucked within the turban of the cap, the long *flamme* was allowed to tumble elegantly about the shoulders when off-duty. Both figures also wear the woollen stable-jacket, with matching waist-pockets of which the left one was simulated for the sake of symmetry. the twin chevrons of lace on the brigadier's cuff proclaim his rank; for brigadiers or sergeants they would be of cloth of the same colour as the lace on the dolman, whereas for more exalted NCOs they would be the equivalent in either silver or gold. The chevron on his left upper-arm represents between eight and ten years' service in the army; his splendid moustache and elegantly fashioned hair attest that those years were certainly all with the light cavalry. It was the custom to intertwine a pistol ball in the ends of the side plaits in order that they might hang at a strict vertical. (Benigni. Courtesy NAM)

sembling a modern poncho, it would be wrapped about the wearer's body or, when on horseback, left to hang about wearer and mount. It was awkward and untidy, and was later replaced by the *manteau-capote*, a long greatcoat with a short shoulder-cape attached, which enabled the wearer to place his crossbelts on the outside of the garment. Both models were entirely dark green. Officers wore similar patterns of cape and greatcoat, but, in addition, generally sported a double-breasted overcoat, or *redingote*, for foot-duty.

Accessories

Boots were the classic Hungarian variety with superior edge bordered with piping of white lace and a tassel, although some varieties were similarly ornamented but in black leather. Troopers generally wore clogs in their place for all fatigue duties. Officers' patterns were identical save that the decorative piping and tassel were of silver; for full dress they sometimes indulged in goatskin versions of red, green or even yellow. Both officers and men used wrist-length white gloves when riding.

Headgear

The variety of hussar shakos is illustrated on p. 32 of *Napoleon's Line Chasseurs*. Around 1802 the 1801-model shako, 190mm tall by 220mm in diameter, lost its *flamme* and detachable peak, and the cockade and plume were removed to the front. Soon after that came the addition of a shako plate placed beneath the cockade; the 1st, 6th and 12th Hussars are recorded with a lozenge-shaped plate out of which the regimental number has been cut. At this period the headgear was maintained in place by a strap which passed beneath the wearer's queue, and a cord was attached to the uniform to prevent

Trooper in campaign dress, 1807. In keeping with the 1791 Regulations, this trooper's 1806 model shako boasts a black plume tipped in the regimental colour. In an equally outdated manner, his shoulderbelts, cartridge-pouch, swordbelt, sabre-tache, sabre and musketoon are all of 1786 pattern, little changed by the 1801 Regulations save that the swordknot is no longer of black leather. Surprising as it may seem, the webbing was supposed to last at least twenty years. (Bitry-Boëly. Courtesy NAM)

P. Benigni.

its loss should it be toppled. Around 1805 these were replaced by chinscales which were universally adopted by the close of 1806. By then the shako had become taller and more bell-shaped and, with the amendments mentioned above, is generally regarded as a model in its own right. Although redundant, shako cords were still employed in a decorative capacity.

A circular dated 9 November 1810 required the final abolition of the shako cords, along with the much-prized tall plumes which were replaced by a simple lentil-shaped pompon; unabashed, the commissary persisted in selling cords and tassels as late as December 1811 and we may be sure that their customers gladly parted with the price of one franc per set.

Further to the 1812 Regulations, an inventory dated 17 September 1812 indicates that shakos of centre companies were to be devoid of the neck-covers folded inside the crown common to models in use at this period. It further informs us that those of elite troops were to be identical to the shakos employed by the grenadiers in the infantry: 10mm taller and wider than that of ordinary troopers, with upper and lower bands and side chevrons of scarlet. Elite troops, however, persisted in wearing their bearskin colpacks till the end of the Empire if they had been previously issued them.

Despite the 1812 Regulations, a new shako made its debut in 1812, the *shako rouleau*. This pattern was somewhat taller than its predecessor; it exceeded 200mm and consisted of a reinforced black felt cylinder, often covered in coloured fabric of which the most popular was red, black leather peak and fold-down neck cover at the rear. The 6th and 8th Hussars are known to have worn it during the Russian campaign of 1812 and, by the end of the Empire, its popularity eclipsed that of the bell-topped shako, although it never made regulation issue.

Off-duty, hussars would sport the *bonnet de police* or, after 1812, the pokalem variety of fatigue-cap; the *bonnets de police*, consisting of a turban and long *flamme* with tassel, were of all combinations of the regimental colours.

Besides their own patterns of all the above headgear, officers also wore a bicorn hat in everyday wear and, particularly in the early years, even on the battlefield.

Brigadier-trompette **and trumpeters in full dress, 1810. Trumpeters were expressly clothed and equipped in such a manner as to make them readily distinguishable from the rank and file. To this end their uniforms were most frequently of inverse colours to those of the men, their schabraques were of black in place of white sheepskin and they were mounted on greys. The NCO is identified by sky blue insignia on his scarlet pelisse. The centre trumpeter's black plume indicates that he belongs to a centre company; his companions' scarlet plumes show that they belong to an elite company. We can conclude that the distribution of the elite symbol, a bearskin colpack, to centre company musicians was an extravagance on the part of the regiment's undoubtedly vain and competitive colonel. (Malespina. Courtesy NAM)**

Trooper in campaign dress, 1807–10. Uncompromisingly demonstrating the reality behind the tinsel of the hussar image, this trooper is entirely clad in uniform and equipment distributed to the hussars between 1806 and 1808. He wears the *Kinski* **tunic, common to the** *chasseurs à cheval*, **as practical and comfortable as the pipe and tobacco hung on the pommel of his sabre is practical and comforting. The sabre is the light-cavalry pattern with copper guard and steel scabbard; it might be either the** *An IX* **or** *An XI* **model, both of which were issued as of 1807. His overalls open laterally by means of eighteen pewter buttons, which can only be seen because the sabretache is missing; it was common practice to leave them at the depot, but they were often lost in the field. (See colour figure B2.) (Benigni. Courtesy NAM)**

Colonel in full dress, 1810. This superior officer wears the officers' pattern of the 1810-model shako, loftier and wider than any preceding example and possessing two further distinguishing features; unlike its predecessor, it reverted to the simple cockade and loop of the 1801 pattern, and, instead of chinscales which were by then universal, it boasted a chinstrap composed of interlocking rings upon a bed of leather. In this instance it is also extravagantly embroidered about the crown. The metal devices visible on his crossbelt were frequently so valuable that many officers were obliged to encase the entire belt and cartridge-pouch in a leather cover when on active service in order to protect their investment. (Rouffet. Courtesy NAM)

Webbing

Comprising swordbelt and slings, sabretache, and the musketoon and cartridge-pouch crossbelts, it conformed to the Decree of 4 *Brumaire An X* (27 October 1801) and was little different from that issued previously save that the swordknot previously of black leather was now of white buff. (See p. 13 of *Napoleon's Line Chasseurs* for specifications, which were identical to those of the hussars.)

The sabretache also differed little from preceding models, the flap usually bearing the regimental number encircled by a wreath of laurel leaves although later models incorporated an Imperial eagle. The flap was covered in cloth of a diversity of colours and the elaborately embroidered motifs were such as to make them almost works of art. Indeed they were so valuable that a leather cover was generally slipped over the flap in order to protect it on the march and in action. Officers often possessed a second, plain, sabretache for wear with everything but parade dress; the embellishment on the flap was confined to either the regimental number alone or a combination of this and a shield or Imperial eagle device of metal. The 1812 Regulations simplified the sabretache to this minimum requirement, but the troops possessing the older versions guarded them jealously and they remained common throughout the Empire.

Edged weapons

Hussars were armed with either the 1786-pattern curved sabre, with copper guard and fittings on the black leather-covered scabbard, or the *An IV* model, with iron hilt and scabbard fittings, in the early years. Around 1807, however, the *An IX* and *An XI* models of light-cavalry sabre began to be distributed, with their distinctive N-shaped copper basket guard and iron scabbard. Officers' patterns were similar save that all copper fittings were gilded. (See *Napoleon's Line Chasseurs* for further detail.)

Firearms

Discounting musketoons of foreign origin with which many hussars were doubtless armed, troopers carried both the 1766 and 1786 models at the dawn of the Empire, along with many others of rather doubtful Republican manufacture. The 1786 pattern is certainly the most frequently represented during the Empire period as a whole, but it gradually gave way to the *An IX* model. The 487mm bayonet which, in principle, accompanied them provides something of an enigma. The author has yet to see a contemporary illustration of a hussar with bayonet fixed or in the bayonet frog of the swordbelt. On reflection, it is perhaps rather difficult to imagine its use as, when it came to close action, the trooper was more likely to rely on his sabre, which was always looped by the swordknot to his right wrist even when he was firing. However, the Regulations of 1 *Vendémiaire An XII* specifically ordered their issue, and records exist from the 1st Hussars, dated January 1808, requesting them. That they were issued is in little doubt and yet no mention is made of them in the 1812 Regulations nor is there a reference to a bayonet-frog in the description of the hussar swordbelt. To confuse the issue, a general inventory of 17 September 1812 refers to '*ceinturons à porte-baïonette*' (swordbelts with bayonet frogs) as items of hussar paraphernalia. They were therefore an item of equipment with which the hussars were certainly supposed to be armed, but whether they actually used them or not and where they kept them is not known.

NCOs', trumpeters' and officers' armament did not include the musketoon, instead they were, in theory, equipped with pistols as firearms. Unfortunately, the holsters with which the Hungarian saddle was fitted were as often as not empty. All hussars were supposedly issued a brace of pistols apiece but even prior to the Empire these were in short supply: those issued included the 1763 model, various patterns 'bodged' together from bits and pieces during the Republic, and antiques dating back to the first half of the 18th century, newly dusted and polished. Excluding those acquired from captured arsenals after 1805, these types remained in service throughout the Empire along with the newer and very scarce *An XIII* model towards the end.

It should be concluded that firearms were seemingly considered a poor second to the sabre as far as the cavalry was concerned, despite their obviously crucial benefit in such instances as the classic impasse of cavalry versus infantry square or even versus fellow cavalry; consider the following revealing extract from an eyewitness' memoirs, referring to an incident at Eylau in 1807:

'Colonel Castex asked if the carbines were loaded . . . he ordered "Present carbines!" . . . and when the Russians [dragoons] were only six paces away the Colonel gave the order, rapidly, "Fire!". The order was executed by the regiment as if on an exercise. The effect of the discharge was terrible: nearly the whole of the first rank of the dragoons was put out of action . . .' (*Souvenirs de Capitaine Parquin*, 1892.)

Admittedly the necessity for reserving fire until the last minute might have had less to do with *sang-froid* than the poor range of the weapon, but well-armed light cavalry were full of potential that had yet to be cultivated and developed. Instead, musketoons and carbines were more readily distributed to the infantry who, in the closing years of the Empire, were desperately short of firearms. Had the masses of cavalry, impotently facing the British squares at Waterloo, been deployed in skirmishing order with pouches full of cartridges and the newly developed rifled carbine, the outcome might have been quite different.

Chef d'escadron in full dress, 1810. Officers' dress reveals a seemingly inexhaustible appetite for lush extravagance. Although initially reserved solely for officers of elite companies, the bearskin colpack proved too delicious a morsel for the tastes of their brother officers to ignore and, by 1808, it was *de rigeur* for every light cavalryman of rank, irrespective of company. This superior officer's sabretache, constructed of scarlet Morocco leather and faced with richly embroidered fabric, has the added embellishment of coiled metal fringes about its perimeter. Such was the expense of these indulgences that most officers possessed two wardrobes, one for full-dress parades and the other for the more serious aspects of their profession. (M.O. Courtesy NAM)

Maréchaux-des-logis of an elite and a centre company in full dress, c.1810. Except for their silver rank chevrons, these NCOs demonstrate full-dress attire for all ranks of hussar. The pelisses were originally to be lined with sheepskin but this proved too difficult and expensive, so it was reserved for the facings alone and the interior was instead lined in white flannel. Note that the toggle and loop affair by which means the pelisse was hung on the shoulder lacks the *raquettes* and tassels with which it is all too frequently illustrated. Although officers' pelisses sometimes bore them, they were bought at personal expense and were by no means an integral part of the garment. (Yvond d'Aubin. Courtesy NAM)

Saddles and Harness

Because of the attractions of the men's costume, horse furniture is generally neglected in most publications and this in turn has led to neglect of the horses themselves and an underestimation of their importance. Indeed they were generally treated better than the men and were certainly more expensive and less easily obtained. Such was the devastating effect of the massive abuse of horseflesh during the Napoleonic Wars that European stocks suffer to this day.

Hussars were mounted on horses of all colours, with musicians having first claim to greys. At the beginning of the Republican Wars, the minimum height for a light cavalry horse was 147cm and, by *An XII*, it was 148cm; but, by their end, stocks were so short that in 1805 Napoleon had to drop the height requirement to 138cm, and this still left the *Grande Armée* short of mounts. With the conquests of large chunks of Europe during the years 1807–13, the army was able to raise the standard to 140cm, but we may be sure that replacements were still a continuous headache considering the numbers of horses necessary to shift the enormous bulk of the *Grande Armée's* cavalry and goods. The proportion of men to horses in the *Grande Armée* of 1812 was 400,000 to 130,000, of which 80,000 were cavalry mounts and 50,000 were draught animals.

This campaign serves as a typical example of hideous wastage. Within the first eight days 8,000 of the beasts had died, and these were the best horses Europe had to offer. After twenty-four days, Murat's cavalry of 22,000 mounted troops was only able to mount 14,000. Such was the exhaustion of the ill-used animals (the French never walked beside their horses, but remained constantly in the saddle), that during the battle of Winkowo, a mere thirty days from the start of the campaign, a great many of the horsemen were obliged to dismount and drag their mounts by the bridle back to their rallying points. At Borodino the casualties numbered 6,000 and worse was to come. Despite six weeks' rest, the retreat from Moscow took a ghastly toll: the first 130km of the way to Smolensk produced the staggering figure of 30,000 losses, which works out at an average of around one

Brigadier in full dress, c.1810. Although dated as late as 1810 by Martinet, this corporal neatly represents the classic hussar stereotype for most of the Empire period, from the top of his 1806-model shako to the tip of his 1786-pattern hussar sabre. He is undoubtedly further armed with a 1786 hussar-pattern musketoon and a brace of 1763-model pistols. In fact, hussars generally left on campaign with only the dolman and breeches or the pelisse and overalls. Frequently, whole detachments would own no more than a dolman and a pair of fatigue overalls apiece in the way of uniform. As to musketoons and pistols: the 1786-pattern musketoon was a highly valued rarity among the preponderance of foreign or Revolutionary-manufactured models (the latter being constructed from a variety of odds and ends). Pistols were in such short supply that were a trooper to receive even one of the pair, he would be lucky if it proved to be the 1763 model; other than that there were only those retrieved from the battlefield, those commandeered from the civilian population or the 'rejuvenated' models dating back to the first half of the 18th century with which the conscripts of 1813 and 1814 were equipped. (Benigni. Courtesy NAM)

cadaver every four metres. Murat's cavalry was reduced to 1,200 horses; thereafter, it is sad to report that the survivors went into the cooking-pot for the most part.

The terrible conditions of the Russian campaign left 200,000 men with 15,000 horses for the campaign of 1813. None of these mounts was saddle-trained and, by the beginning of hostilities, it is estimated that only 3,000 were at all suitable as cavalry mounts. This shortage of cavalry undoubtedly cost France the Empire.

The horse furniture was of Hungarian pattern and has been extensively illustrated and documented in *Napoleon's Line Chasseurs*. It consisted of a wooden tree with a suspended seat and a sheepskin schabraque trimmed in scalloped lace of the regimental colour. The wooden tree was naturally extremely hard, and many good animals' backs

Trumpeter in full dress, 1810. An interesting figure with light blue pelisse, breeches, facings, and *flamme* on his white colpack. His dolman is scarlet, as is his plume, designating his elite-company status. The horse furniture is unusual in that in place of the sheepskin schabraque one associates with other ranks, he possesses a scarlet cloth schabraque and matching woollen portmanteau, both edged in white lace. (Benigni. Courtesy NAM)

were permanently damaged by the negligent use of too thin a horse blanket. Although there was one veterinary surgeon per 500 head, the falling standard of trained riders in the later years, combined with the fact that the mounts were badly broken-in, resulted in the observation that a new detachment of cavalry was most immediately recognizable by the pungent odour of the horses' suppurating saddle sores. Attached to the tree were a pair of leather pistol-holsters, a leather case for pocketing spare shoes and natural-leather straps for securing the portmanteau, greatcoat and musketoon in position. The portmanteau was a cylindrical valise strapped behind the cantle, the round ends were edged in lace and often bore the regimental number. The Hungarian-style bridle was composed of black leather with white metal and copper fittings.

Officers' horse furniture was similar save that the tree boasted leather side-panels, pommel and cantle were covered in Morocco leather matching the schabraque, bronzed spurs and pistol-holsters were tipped in gold- or silver-plate. Although examples of schabraques with a false seat of black sheepskin are known, the most common were entirely of cloth, reinforced with leather at the girth. In everyday use, a plain schabraque with piping of coloured goats' hair was employed, but, for more formal occasions, superior officers would adopt the leopard-skin schabraque; while their subordinates utilised the standard cloth variety, trimmed with lace and ornamented with devices in the corners. The 1812 Regulations regularised the excesses thus: a 50mm-wide lace about the perimeter of the cloth for colonels and majors, with a concentric lace of 15mm-width within it, of identical colour for colonels but of opposite colour for majors; a single strip of 50mm-width for *chef d'escadrons*; a 45mm-strip for captains; and single strips of 40mm and 35mm for lieutenants and second-lieutenants respectively. The corners of the schabraque were to bear the regimental number inscribed in lace to a height of 80mm. The portmanteau came in for equally precise treatment with the decorative lace confined to a 35mm-width for superior officers, 20mm for all others, and the regimental number no taller than 35mm.

In closing the sections on dress, equipment and horse furniture it is important to stress that in the first instance hussars travelled without the encumbrance of their entire kit, leaving the depots on campaign in either dolman or pelisse and riding breeches or overalls. Secondly, it should not be assumed that the hussars were ever as fully equipped as official inventories of available stocks might suggest, the regiments did not dispose of unlimited funds and a fully equipped regiment was not only a rarity but probably a myth. Inspection reports for the year 1809 indicate arriving detachments joining the *Grande Armée* with combinations of the following dress: dolman and breeches; dolman and overalls; some in pelisses; others in fatigue overalls, and a very few with both breeches and overalls. The classic fully dressed and fully armed hussar of popular imagination, all too frequently repeated in print, is a figure, therefore, belonging more to the theatre than the battlefield.

War Records and Regimental Histories

The 1st Hussars

Regimental history:

1720: Raised by and named after Count Ladislas-Ignace de Bercheny in Turkey.

1791: Renamed the 1er Régiment de Hussards.

1814: Became the Régiment de Hussards du Roi.

1815: Renamed the 1er Régiment de Hussards and disbanded later that same year.

War record:

1805: With the Grande Armée at Ulm and Austerlitz.

1806–7: With the Grande Armée at Jena, Eylau, Friedland and Heilsberg.

1808–12: With the Armées d'Espagne and du Portugal at Braga, Santillo, Sabugal and Monasterio.

1813: The 1st Squadron served with the Grande Armée at Jüterbock, Leipzig and Hanau.

1814: Part of the Armée d'Italie: Mincio.

1815: Engaged at Namur.

The 2nd Hussars

Regimental history:

1735: Created partly of Hungarian volunteers in Strasbourg on 25 January, and named Chamborant.

Lieutenant of the elite company in full dress, 1810–12. This individual, though elegantly dressed, is considerably more soberly attired than most of the officers seen so far. Aside from his comparatively low rank, the reason could be that, having hit a peak of outlandish costume between 1809 and 1810, hussar officers were at last beginning to dress more modestly for both financial and practical reasons. Indeed, as early as 1810 an official circular was issued simplifying the headdress of officers of centre companies by prohibiting (albeit without any immediately noticeable effect) all cords, *raquettes*, tassels and plumes; further, Bardin's motive for the rationalisation of officers' and other ranks' dress in the 1812 Regulations was to curb the enormous expense inherent in a wardrobe so cluttered with unnecessary items of dress and equipment. Finally, five continuous years of warfare obliged even the officers to cut down on baggage, which doubtless accounts for this officer's simple scarlet schabraque devoid even of embroidered devices in the angles. (Vallet. Courtesy NAM)

1791: Renamed the 2eme Régiment de Hussards.

1814: Became the Régiment de Hussards de la Reine.

1815: Renamed the 2eme Régiment de Hussards and disbanded in September of that year.

War record:

1805–8: With the Grande Armée at Austerlitz, Halle, Crewitz, Mohrungen, Osterode and Friedland.

Brigadiers of a centre and an elite company in full dress, 1810–12. The two major points of interest in these figures are the shako of the NCO on the left and both their rank insignia. The centre company *brigadier* has acquired what has now been dubbed the 1810-model shako: officially described on 9 November of that year as a towering 220mm in height and 270mm in diameter; it is thought to have actually been somewhat smaller and narrower. It bore the distinctive Imperial eagle posed on a semi-circle as a cut-out plate. Turning to the rank insignia: despite the fact that the NCOs reviewed so far have had chevrons of the same colour as their uniform lace, both of these individuals' chevrons are scarlet. Although there are some other instances of this in other regiments, there is seemingly no explanation for it. (Boisselier. Courtesy NAM)

1808–13: Saw service in the Peninsula: Medellin, Alcabon, Ronda, Sierra de Cazala, Gebora, Los Santos, Albufera and Somanis.
1813: With the Grande Armée at Leipzig.
1814: Fought at Montereau.
1815: Attached to the Corps d'Observation du Jura: defence of Belfort.

The 3rd Hussars

Regimental history:
1764: Created by and named after Count Esterhazy, and formed from a squadron from each of the Bercheny, Chamborant and Nassau hussars.
1791: Renamed the 3eme Régiment de Hussards.
1814: Became the Régiment de Hussards du Dauphin.
1815: Renamed the 3eme Régiment de Hussards and disbanded later that same year.

War record:
1805–7: With the Grande Armée at Ulm, Jena, Magdebourg, Gollup, Bartenstein, Langenheim, Hoff and Guttstadt.
1808–13: Service in the Peninsula: Tudela, Astorga, Tanoris, Baños, Tamanies, Alba-de-Tormes, Ciudad-Rodrigo, Almeida, Leria, Alcoluto, Redinha, Fuentes d'Onoro, Los Arapilos and Vittoria.
1813: With the Grande Armée at Leipzig.
1814: Fought at Brienne, Montereau and Sézanne.
1815: Engaged at Belfort.

The 4th Hussars

Regimental history:
1783: Created by Royal Ordonnance of 31 July for the Duc de Chartres, for whom the title of Colonel-Général of Hussars was created in 1779. Formed from one squadron from each of the Bercheny, Chamborant, Conflans and Esterhazy hussars, and named Colonel-Général.
1791: Renamed the 5eme Régiment de Hussards.
1793: Became the 4eme Régiment de Hussards by Convention Decree of 4 June when the original 4eme Régiment (ex-Hussards de Saxe) emigrated.

1814: Renamed the Régiment de Hussards de Monsieur.
1815: Renamed the 4eme Régiment de Hussards and disbanded in September of that same year.

War record:
1805: With the Grande Armée at Austerlitz.

Brigadier-fourrier in full dress, 1811–12. Having noted his curious way of tucking his shako's chinscales out of the way, this quarter-master corporal is of interest for his rank insignia: typical *brigadier's* twin chevrons at the cuff, but a distinctive diagonal strip of lace where we might more readily expect service chevrons on his left upper-arm. (Van Huen. Courtesy NAM)

Trooper in campaign dress, Spain, 1811–12. Probably return-
ing from a foraging expedition, the proceeds of which we can
see slung beneath the portmanteau of his saddle, this casually-
clad hussar's shako sports a rough cloth cover, tied in bows at
the rear, and a lentil-shaped pompon of red with a white
centre. Note the water gourd of brown leather slung over his
right shoulder and tucked beneath his left arm. (Benigni.
Courtesy NAM)

Maréchal-des-logis, sapper, 1810–12. Cavalry regiments generally numbered only farriers among their effectives—apart
from the dragoons whose sappers were a tradition carried over
from their mounted infantry origins—but hussar regiments
were recorded with sappers among the ranks in several
instances. The voluminous beard and crossed-axe devices on
their sleeves were hallmarks of their trade, along with the
flaming grenade symbol universal to elite troops. This
individual's rank is indicated by the chevrons above the cuffs
and the single chevron on the left upper-arm, all of silver lace on
a scarlet ground. (Van Huen. Courtesy NAM)

1806–7: Remained with the Grande Armée: Schleiz,
Jena, Lübeck, Liebstadt and Mohrungen.
1808–13: With the Armée d'Espagne at Alcanitz,
Belchite, Stella, Chiclana, Sagonte, Yecla and the
Ordal Pass.
1813: With the 3eme Corps de Cavalerie of the Grande
Armée at Gross-Beeren and Leipzig.
1814: Part of the 6eme Corps de Cavalerie of the Armée
de Lyon at Lons-le-Saulnier, Saint-Georges and
Lyon.
1815: Fought at Ligny and Waterloo.

The 5th Hussars

Regimental history:

1783: Created by Ordonnance of 14 September from the
cavalry of the Légion de Lauzun (formed in 1778 and
newly returned from the American War of Inde-
pendence) and named the Lauzun hussars.
1791: Became the 6eme Régiment de Hussards.
1793: Renamed the 5eme Régiment de Hussards by
Decree of 4 June.
1814: Became the Régiment de Hussards d'Angoulême.
1815: Renamed the 5eme Régiment de Hussards and
disbanded on 1 November.

War record:

1805–7: With the Grande Armée at Austerlitz, Crewitz,
Golymin, Watterdorf, Stettin, Eylau, Heilsberg and
Königsberg.
1809: Part of the Armée d'Allemagne at Eckmühl and
Wagram.
1812: With the Grande Armée at Borodino, Winkowo
and the Berezina.
1813: With the Grande Armée at Bautzen, Leipzig and
Hanau.
1814: Fought at Arcis-sur-Aube.
1815: With the Armée du Nord at Ligny, Waterloo and
Versailles.

The 6th Hussars

Regimental history:

1792: Created as the 7eme Régiment de Hussards by
Convention Decree of 23 November from the Boyer
light horse (a freecorps alternatively known as the
Hussards Défenseurs de la Liberté et de l'Egalité
raised in September of 1792).

P. Benigni

Trumpeter in campaign dress, Spain, 1811–12. This interesting figure wears a scarlet dolman, faced in sky blue, and sky blue overalls with seams reinforced in scarlet lace. Note the twin chevrons on his left upper-arm which proclaim between sixteen and twenty years' service. He is armed with a 1786-pattern hussar sabre and, tucked into the schabraque strap on his left, a 1763-model pistol. The horse furniture consists of a brown sheepskin schabraque, Hungarian saddle, on an ochre saddle-blanket trimmed in blue, and harness embellished with tassels of mixed threads of yellow, red and blue. (Bucquoy. Courtesy NAM)

1793: Renumbered by Decree of 4 June as the 6eme Régiment de Hussards.
1814: Renamed the Régiment de Hussards de Berry.
1815: Renamed the 6eme Régiment de Hussards and disbanded that same year.

War record:
1805: With the Grande Armée at Ulm and Altenmarkt.

1809: With the Armée d'Italie at La Piave, Raab and Wagram.
1812: With the Grande Armée at Krasnoe, Smolensk and Borodino.
1813: Part of the Grande Armée at Möckern, Lützen, Bautzen, Reichenbach, Dresden and Leipzig.
1814: Fought at La Rothière, Champaubert, Vauchamps, Athies, Reims, La Fére-Champenoise and Paris.
1815: With the Armée de Nord at Ligny and Rocquencourt.

The 7th Hussars

Regimental history:
1792: Formed at Compiègne further to the Convention Decree of 23 November, the regiment was initially dubbed the Hussards de Lamothe before becoming the 8eme Régiment de Hussards.
1793: Renumbered the 7eme Régiment de Hussards following the Decree of 4 June.
1794: Augmented by the cavalry of the Légion de Kellermann (into which the 4th Squadron of the Régiment Saxe-Hussards (No. 4) had been drafted upon the regiment's defection).
1814: Renamed the Régiment de Hussards d'Orléans.
1815: Became the Colonel-Général Hussards prior to being renamed the 7eme Régiment de Hussards. Disbanded in November of that same year.

War record:
1805: Part of the III Corps of the Grande Armée at Mariazell, Afflenz and Austerlitz.
1806–7: With the Grande Armée at Gera, Zehdenick, Prentzlow, Stettin, Lübeck, Czenstowo, Golymin, Eylau, Heilsberg and Königsberg.
1809: With the Armée d'Allemagne at Peising, Ratisbonne, Raab, Wagram and Znaïm.
1812: With the Grande Armée at Vilna, Smolensk, Ostrowno, Borodino, Winkowo and Malojaroslavetz.
1813: Remained with the Grande Armée: Borna, Altenbourg, Leipzig and Hanau.
1814: Fought at Vauchamps, Montereau, Reims, Laon and Paris.
1815: With the Armée du Nord at Fleurus and Waterloo.

The 8th Hussars

Regimental history:
1793: Formed from the Eclaireurs de l'Armée (organised in October 1792 at Nancy by Colonel Fabrefonds) further to the Convention Decree of 26 February, and named the 9eme Régiment de Hussards. Renamed the 8eme Régiment de Hussards by the 4 June decree that same year.

1 Sous-lieutenant, 2nd Hussars, campaign dress, 1805
2 Trooper, 2nd Hussars, full dress, 1801-2
3 Trumpeter, 4th Hussars, full dress, 1804-5

ANGUS McBRIDE

A

1 Lieutenant, 1st Hussars, service dress, 1805-7
2 Trooper, 1st Hussars, campaign dress, 1806-8
3 Trumpeter, 5th Hussars, full dress, 1805

ANGUS McBRIDE

1 Major, 8th Hussars, service dress, c. 1809
2 Trooper, 9th Hussars, full dress, 1809
3 Trumpeter, 5th Hussars, service dress, 1808-12

ANGUS McBRIDE

C

1 Lieutenant, 6th Hussars, service dress, c.1810
2 Brigadier-fourrier, 7th Hussars, campaign dress, 1807-8
3 Trumpet-major, 4th Hussars, campaign dress, c.1810

ANGUS McBRIDE

1 Captain, 4th Hussars, full dress, 1810
2 Sapper, 5th Hussars, campaign dress, 1813
3 Trumpeter, 6th Hussars, campaign dress, 1812

ANGUS McBRIDE

E

1 Chef d'escadron, 5th Hussars, campaign dress, 1810-12
2 Sapper, 1st Hussars, full dress, 1810-12
3 Trumpeter, 9th (bis) Hussars, campaign dress, 1812-13

ANGUS McBRIDE

1 Captain, 3rd Hussars, full dress, 1809-13
2 Brigadier, 12th Hussars, full dress, 1813-14
3 Trumpeter, 1st Hussars, service dress, 1812

1 Lieutenant, 6th Hussars, service dress, 1814
2 Marechal-des-logis, 4th Hussars, full dress, 1813-14
3 Trumpeter, 2nd Hussars, full dress, 1812-14

H

1814: Disbanded on 12 May.

War record:

1805: With the Grande Armée at Memmingen, Aicha and Austerlitz.

1806–7: Part of the Grande Armée at Jena, Fakembourg, Eylau and the passage of the Passarge.

1809: With the Armée d'Allemagne at Ratisbonne, Essling, Enzersdorf, Wagram and Znaïm.

1801–11: Attached to the Armée de Brabant in Holland.

1812–13: With the Grande Armée at Ostrowno, Vilna, Borodino, Magdebourg, Altenbourg and Leipzig.

1814: Engaged in the defences of Danzig and Strasbourg and the action at Champaubert.

The 9th Hussars

Regimental history:

1793: Created by the Convention Decree of 25 March as the 10eme Régiment de Hussards from the 2eme Corps of the Hussards de la Liberté (themselves created by the Decree of 2 September 1792). Further to the Convention Decree of 4 June, the regiment was renamed the 9eme Régiment de Hussards.

1814: Disbanded on 12 May.

War record:

1805: With the Grande Armée at Wertingen, Amstetten, Wischau and Austerlitz.

1806–7: Part of the Grande Armée at Saalfeld, Jena, Pultusk, Stettin, Ostrolenka, Danzig, Heilsberg and Friedland.

1809: With the Armée d'Allemagne at Eckmühl, Essling, Raab and Wagram.

1810–13: In Spain: Barbastro and Valencia.

1812–13: With the Grande Armée's 2eme Corps de Réserve at Borodino and Mojaïsk.

1813: With the II Corps of the Grande Armée at Bautzen, Reichenbach, Wachau, Leipzig and Hanau.

1814: Took part in the defence of Schlestadt.

The 10th Hussars

Regimental history:

1793: Formed from the Hussards Noirs (also called the Hussards de la Mort), a freecorps organised in the Nord département, and named the 10eme Régiment de Hussards.

1814: Disbanded at Fontenay on 1 August.

War record:

1805: Part of the V Corps of the Grande Armée at Wertingen, Elchingen, Ulm, Braunau, Amstetten, Vienna, Hollabrünn and Austerlitz.

1806–7: With the Grande Armée at Saalfeld, Jena, Stettin and Pultusk.

1809–11: With the V Corps in Spain: Magalon, Perdiguera, Licinera, Saragossa, Ocaña, Badajoz, Gebora and Albufera.

1813: With the Grande Armée at Weissenfels, Lützen, Bautzen, Dessau, Wachau and Leipzig.

1814: Engaged at La Rothière, Montmirail, Craonne and Laon.

The 11th Hussars

Regimental history:

1793: Formed at Amboise 26 June from various freecorps units including the cuirassiers of the Légion Germanique (created in 1792) and named the 11eme Régiment de Hussards.

1803: Became the 29eme Régiment de Dragons.

Sous-lieutenant **in campaign dress, 1811–13. This courier's spring uniform, recorded in Spain, consists of an officers'-pattern 1810-model shako, in theory 220mm tall and 270mm in diameter, standard dolman and scarlet zouave-style overalls. His cartridge-pouch crossbelt is encased in a crimson leather cover and his ornate full-dress sabretache is replaced by a plain leather version bearing an eagle device. His armament comprises an** *An XI*-**pattern officers' sabre and a brace of pistols. (Benigni. Courtesy NAM)**

Colonel Merlin in full dress, 1812–13. Magnificently turned out for dress parade, this colonel has reverted to the shako in place of the fashionable bearskin colpack: it is the *shako rouleau*, or cylindrical shako. Taller still than the 1810-pattern bell-topped shako, it made its appearance in 1812 and, despite being a non-regulation model, it was widely worn throughout the remaining years of the Empire. As we can see, the pelisse was at this point very short indeed, in contrast to the early patterns. The dolman was of correspondingly short cut and the barrel-sash consequently mounted very high on the waist. (Benigni. Courtesy NAM)

1810: Recreated from the 2eme Régiment de Hussards Hollandais as the 11eme Régiment de Hussards.
1814: Disbanded.

War record:
1805–11: See *Napoleon's Dragoons and Lancers*, p. 34.
1812–13: With the Grande Armée at Borodino, Krasnoe, Berezina, Leipzig and Hanau.

The 12th Hussars

Regimental history:
1794: Formed 9 February from the Hussards de la Montagne, a freecorps created at Bayonne in 1793.
1803: Became the 30eme Régiment de Dragons on 20 September.
1813: Re-formed 17 February from the 9eme (bis) Régiment de Hussards. The 9eme (bis) had been created 8 January 1812 from three squadrons of the 9th Hussars detached in Spain.
1814: Disbanded.

War record:
1805–11: See *Napoleon's Dragoons and Lancers*, pp. 34–5.
1812–13: With the Armée d'Aragon at Barbastro, Diar and Borga.
1813: Three squadrons were with the Grande Armée at Gross-Beeren, Medergersdorf, Leipzig and Hanau.
1814: With the Armée de Lyon at Mâcon, Limonest and Saint-Donat.

The 13th Hussars*

Regimental history:
1795: Formed 1 September from the Hussards des Alpes, a freecorps created on 31 January.
1796: Disbanded.
1813: Re-formed following the Imperial Decree of 28 January with recruits from Rome and Tuscany (*départements* of France at this point). Regiment was

* The appellation of 13eme Régiment de Hussards was also applied to the Légion Franche de Cavalerie des Americains et du Midi from its creation on 7 September 1792. The Convention Decree of 21 February 1793 named the unit the 13eme Régiment de Chasseurs à Cheval.

Trumpeter in full dress, 1813. This figure illustrates the hussar trumpeters' full-dress uniform as prescribed by the 1812 Regulations. The Imperial Livery he wears was in fact decreed as early as 1810 in an effort to standardise the dress of musicians of all arms, thereby curbing the worst excesses of inter-regimental rivalry for best-dressed heads of column. Needless to say, in the hussars the order was either politely ignored altogether or grudgingly obeyed till the fuss died down, at which point the brand-new livery was deemed worn out and replaced by the colonel's latest creation. Certainly, the trumpet banner illustrated here never got further than the designer's desk; but the Imperial Livery itself is known to have been issued. (Bitry-Boëly. Courtesy NAM)

then dissolved on 13 December and the men integrated into the 14eme Régiment de Hussards.
1814: Re-formed 1 January from the Régiment de Hussards Jérôme-Napoléon, created 5 August 1813. The regiment was finally dissolved on 12 August.

War record:
1813: With the Grande Armée at Belzig, Lubnitz and Leipzig.
1813: Part of the Armée d'Italie at Viareggio and Livornia.

The 14th Hussars

Regimental history:

1813: Raised in Turin further to the Imperial Decree of 28 January and formed of recruits from Genoa and Piedmont. Disbanded on 11 November following the Allies' violation of the capitulation of Dresden. The regiment was then re-formed on 13 December in Turin from dissolved units of the 13th and 14th Hussars.

1814: Disbanded on 16 July.

War record:

1813: Engaged in the defence of Dresden as part of the Grande Armée.

1814: Attached to the Armée d'Italie.

The Plates

A1 Sous-lieutenant of the 2nd Hussars in campaign dress, 1805

Recorded by Baron Lejeune, a contemporary of the period, this is an officer in very typical service dress. Although issued a multitude of different uniform and equipment items, hussars were rarely anything like fully accoutred and, even in the instance of an officer personally purchasing his additional uniforms, he would leave all but necessaries behind him at the depot. The figure from which this illustration is drawn is mounted, with a black bearskin schabraque edged in scalloped light blue lace. (Illustration after Benigni)

A2 Trooper of the 2nd Hussars in full dress, 1801–2

Formed in 1802, the single elite company of each regiment was accorded a bearskin in imitation of grenadiers of infantry. This interesting early model is literally a fur-covered shako which this regiment retained in use as late as 1805. Only this individual's cords and tassels inform us as to the occasion, he might otherwise be in marching order;

Hussars in stable dress and overcoat, 1813. The left-hand trooper, in stable-jacket of green wool, wears a light blue fatigue-cap in place of the old *bonnet de police*. Dubbed the 'pokalem' cap, it had the benefit of side flaps which folded down to cover the ears and button under the chin. His companion's greatcoat is equally new in design, consisting of a button-up coat and short shoulder-cape combined, it was far removed from its predecessor, an immense green cloak equipped with a hood. The earlier model would be either wound about the body or left to fall from the shoulders; this looked tolerable on horseback, but on foot the wearer resembled a bundle of laundry. (Benigni. Courtesy NAM)

whole detachments are known to have left for campaign without overalls, waistcoats or dolmans, such being the strain on funds and distribution. His horse's schabraque was of white sheepskin trimmed in sky blue. His lance is a most irregular and unusual form of armament. (Illustration after Rousselot/Cottreau Coll.)

A3 Trumpeter of the 4th Hussars in full dress, 1804–5

Drawn from German sources this trumpeter's dress is confirmed by an entry in the Marckolsheim MS for 1807–8 in all respects save the headgear. Unusual for so late a date, we can see that his 1801-model shako retains its *flamme*, an accessory which was universal to the headgear's predecessors but

Sapper in service dress, 1814. Retaining his prized colpack in the face of the 1812 Regulations which prescribed an infantry-style grenadier's shako for elite light cavalry, this business-like fellow is armed with the old 1786 hussar-pattern musketoon. His colpack's *flamme* would usually be tucked within the bearskin and covered with a leather top for the march. Note the red-trimmed black sheepskin schabraque instead of the white one reserved for all but musicians. (Benigni. Courtesy NAM)

29

Trumpeter in service dress, 1814. He wears a scarlet cloth-covered *shako rouleau*, white pelisse and red trousers with a strip of white lace down the outer seams. Initially these were overalls with side openings; trousers had by now become a garment rather than an accessory and had ceased to be fastened along the outer-leg, but rather by means of a button-fly concealed behind a wide flap at the front. The trim on the schabraque is light blue and the red woollen portmanteau is edged in white. The trumpet cords are of mixed red and yellow threads. (Benigni. Courtesy NAM)

which began to be omitted around 1802. The trumpeter of 1807–8 is similar except that he wears an 1806-model shako, covered in red cloth, bearing a lozenge-shaped shako plate out of which the regimental number has been cut. The trumpeter illustrated is the earliest recorded Empire musician of this regiment. (Illustration after Rousselot)

B1 Lieutenant of the 1st Hussars in service dress, 1805–7
In contrast to the manner in which they are most frequently represented, hussars wore either the dolman or the pelisse except on full dress occasions on which the pelisse would be slung on the left shoulder. Prior to the introduction of chinscales in 1805, a leather strap was looped beneath the queue of the wearer in order to maintain the headgear in position. This individual's horse furniture comprises sky blue schabraque and portmanteau edged in silver lace. (Illustration after Rousselot)

B2 Trooper of the 1st Hussars in campaign dress, 1806–8
The black and white illustrations in this title are all of the 1st Hussars and readers are referred to the illustration on p. 13 for details of this interesting figure's costume and equipment. (Illustration after Benigni)

B3 Trumpeter of the 5th Hussars in full dress, 1805
The 5th Hussars were the ex-Lauzun Hussars to whom, among others, Hoffmann ascribes red facings at their transformation date of 1793 from the 6th Hussars. Thus, although the 5th Hussars are recorded as having sky blue uniform faced in sky blue and white, the red uniform is quite correct and authenticated, being of inverse colours to that of the troopers, in the popular fashion, despite its seeming inaccuracy. The regiment is known to have briefly experimented with a red dolman for troopers around 1802. (Illustration after Jean/Kolbe)

Trumpeter of an elite company in service dress, 1814–15. Unusually, his white bearskin colpack bears a sky blue plume in place of the scarlet one we might expect of an elite cavalryman; additionally, the headgear's *flamme* is of the same colour, instead of the familiar red. His pelisse is white with crimson braid. His red trousers are the new kind already described, and were adopted by many regiments for even full dress wear. Some varieties were reinforced with leather on the inside leg in identical manner to the laterally opening overalls, retaining in some instances a small set of buttons at the cuff to facilitate their wear over the tall Hungarian boot; those without leather protection were constructed with a double layer of material to prevent wear and tear. The trumpet cord and tassels are red. (Benigni. Courtesy NAM)

P. Benigni.

C1 Major of the 8th Hussars in service dress, c. 1809
Majors of all branches of the *Grande Armée* were distinguished by a highly individual method: they wore identical insignia to that of the colonel of their regiment, except for the opposite lace colour to that employed by the rest of the regiment. If this figure were, for example, a major of the 7th Hussars (whose uniform was of the same colours but whose lace colour was yellow) we would see gold lace where here we have silver and vice versa. (Reconstruction)

C2 Trooper of the 9th Hussars in full dress, 1809
This rear view allows us the opportunity to describe the barrel-sash's composition: an unravelled total length of 260cm, it consisted of fifty doubled-over lengths of crimson wool, which were divided into two equal groups of 25 doubled lengths, and then threaded in pairs through a total of nine mobile cylindrical barrels, which prevented the lateral opening-out of the threads. Each end of the belt was permanently secured by immovable barrels; to one end was attached a doubled-over length of cord which terminated in a pair of tassels and had a series of four fixed crimson knots along its length, the last being 10cm from the twin tassels; to the other extremity was fixed another, though considerably shorter, doubled-over cord, terminating in a 4cm-long toggle about which the looped end of the long cord was fastened. The free end of the long cord was then knotted loosely about itself after having been slipped through the threads of the front of the sash. (Illustration after Girbal)

C3 Trumpeter of the 5th Hussars in service dress, elite company
This second trumpeter of the 5th Hussars (see B3) probably dates from between 1808 and 1812. He wears a No. 2 dress, long-tailed *surtout*, with the unusual addition of lapels, strongly reminiscent of the infantry officers' pattern 1812 *habit-veste*. His

Lieutenant of an elite company in campaign dress, 1814. In place of the prescribed infantry grenadier-pattern shako, with scarlet bands and chevrons, and the cylindrical shako of his troop, this officer favours the non-regulation bearskin colpack. Notice the Morocco leather cover protecting both his crossbelt and cartridge-pouch. On the march, and in action generally, the decorative features of dress such as plume, cords and *raquettes* were packed in the portmanteau. His horse furniture comprises a cloth schabraque embroidered with an Hungarian knot and equipped with a black bearskin cover atop the pistol holsters. (Benigni. Courtesy NAM)

Colonel Clary in full dress, 1814. The colonel is attired and accoutred in similar style to his predecessors save that the uniform has progressed a stage further, moving away from the classic hussar look, with the inclusion of trousers in the full-dress wardrobe. In the space of less than ten years the costume had developed from a style that had remained unchanged for virtually a century in its rigid conformity to its classical origins, to one that incorporated the comforts and requirements of civilian fashion. (Benigni. Courtesy NAM)

schabraque and portmanteau are sky blue and edged in yellow lace. The blue shako was adopted in 1808 and replaced in 1813 by a scarlet cylindrical pattern. Strange to say, the regiment at this point had trumpeters dressed in both the scarlet-influenced manner shown here and in the modernised inverse-colours: consisting of white dolman, sky blue facings and sky blue pelisse and breeches. (Illustration after Jean/Kolbe)

P. Benedini.

34

D1 Lieutenant of the 6th Hussars in service dress, c. 1810
Reconstructed from existing garments, among other sources, this officer in marching order typifies the no-nonsense approach to practical campaign dress. His shako is his sole real extravagance and would doubtless be covered in a black oilskin cover at the least sign of inclement weather. Note that the overalls now open by means of a front fly concealed behind a flap in similar manner to the riding breeches, our first indication of the development of trousers as a garment in their own right thus far. (Reconstruction from existing relics, a contemporary portrait and Baldauf)

D2 Brigadier-fourrier of the 7th Hussars in campaign dress, 1807–8
The quarter-master corporal was nominally in charge of the collective quarter-masters of each company of the regiment. Numbering a total of eight in a four-squadron regiment, their rank conferred upon them the organisational responsibilities of distributing food and drink, as well as billets to the members of their respective companies. The status of *fourrier* proper was indicated by a single diagonal strip of metal lace the same colour as the buttons on the left upper arm, subsequent rank was designated by chevrons above the cuff in the normal manner. Note his *charivari* pattern overalls, complete with twin hip-pockets. (Reconstruction)

D3 Trumpet-major of the 4th Hussars in campaign dress in Spain, c. 1810
This trumpet-major, a *maréchal-des-logis* in rank, occupied a highly privileged position next to the regiment's colonel, from whose side he would never stray in order that he might translate the officer's orders instantaneously into trumpet calls that would then be communicated in turn to the troops by the company trumpeters under his command. The role of trumpeter should not be interpreted as 'musician' since they fulfilled a signals role in an era

Trumpeter in full dress, 1815. This colourful musician's dress comprises a red *shako rouleau* with yellow pompon and white plume, a sky blue dolman with red cuffs and a white pelisse. The shako trim and cords are composed of mixed white and crimson threads, as are the lace and braid on the dolman and pelisse, the colours of the Bourbon livery lace. Further testimony to the brief return of France's monarchy is the fleur-de-lis device on the sabretache. (Benigni. Courtesy NAM)

ignorant of radio waves. Trumpeters received the billets of NCOs and double the pay of a trooper, and it will therefore be appreciated that this individual's rank of sergeant belied his true, considerably higher status. (Illustration after Rousselot/contemporary Spanish illustration)

E1 Captain of the 4th Hussars in full dress, 1810
This high-ranking full-dress figure is of the classic hussar appearance we have endeavoured to avoid, but is no less worthy of comment for that. The alternating chevrons of rank measured 14mm and 23mm respectively, and the bearskin colpack, initially reserved solely for officers of elite companies, was by this time widely adopted by officers generally, irrespective of company. Note the

Hussars in campaign dress, 1814. The leading trooper is armed with the outdated 1786 hussar-pattern musketoon, 103cm in overall length, and the *An XI* light-cavalry sabre, the blade of which was fully 845mm long. Note the fashion of slinging the *manteau-capote 'en sautoir'* about the right shoulder instead of strapping it forward of the saddle's pommel beneath the schabraque; this afforded the wearer some protection from cut and thrust weapons. (Benigni. Courtesy NAM)

grenade-shaped plume holder at its top. (Illustration after Hoffmann/Martinet)

E2 Sapper of the 5th Hussars in campaign dress, 1813
The dolman of this colourful figure would have been sky blue with matching collar and white cuffs, and its left upper-arm would bear identical devices to those indicated on the pelisse. His sheepskin schabraque was white with sky blue trim and portmanteau. His most interesting feature is the crossed-axe device on the sabretache; but note also the cuffs on his overalls, cut high in imitation of Hungarian boots. (Illustration after contemporary illustration)

E3 Trumpeter of the 6th Hussars in campaign dress, 1812
The leather reinforcements to his overalls have developed to such an extent that only a tiny area of the base cloth remains visible. A further unusual feature is the white fur of the bearskin and pelisse; relatively common in the early Empire, it was at this period a luxurious rarity. His schabraque is of black sheepskin, trimmed in scarlet, with a portmanteau of light blue, edged in yellow. (Illustration after Hesse/Marckolsheim MS)

F1 Chef d'escadron of the 5th Hussars in campaign dress, 1810–12
Created in 1793, the title of *chef d'escadron* replaced that of lieutenant-colonel and, until the innovation of a major, was second only to the *chef de brigade* or colonel. During the Empire there were supposedly three officers of such rank within each hussar regiment. In summer service uniform, this superior officer's horse furniture would consist of sky blue schabraque and portmanteau, both liberally edged in gold lace of 50mm and 35mm in width respectively. (Illustration after Rousselot)

F2 Sapper of the 1st Hussars in full dress, 1810–12
This elite trooper, his enormous beard and crossed-axe patches defining his status of sapper, would ride at the head of the column along with the regimental eagle, forming with his fellow *sapeurs* a guard of honour about the standard for both parades and battlefield engagements. The fact that hussar regiments rather surprisingly numbered sappers in their ranks, in no way precluded them from counting the more conventional farriers among

Colonel Oudinot in full dress, 1815. The return of Louis XVIII in 1814 heralded the transformation of the leading regiments of each branch of the army into a king's regiment, thus Colonel Oudinot commanded the *Hussards du Roi* at the time of Napoleon's return for the Hundred Days' Campaign. While royalist emblems such as the white cockade were certainly replaced by Imperial equivalents during the unhappy campaign, it is extremely doubtful that such expensive items as officers' accoutrements, emblazoned as here with royal arms and fleur-de-lis, could have been. Uniforms at Waterloo must consequently have frequently borne royalist devices. (Benigni. Courtesy NAM)

Trooper of an elite company and *maréchal-des-logis* of a centre company in full dress, 1815. The dress of the last hussars of the Empire period is a pleasing amalgam of 18th- and 19th-century costume. The higher-waisted and slimmer cut of the uniform, combined with the *shako rouleau's* height and style, lends the dress a modern air which contrasts with the plaited and queued hair and outmoded equipment. (Benigni. Courtesy NAM)

P. Benigni.

them as well; given the title of *maréchal-ferrant*, their status was indicated by a scarlet horseshoe upon either the upper left or right sleeve. (Illustration after Bucquoy)

F3 Trumpeter of the 9th (bis) Hussars in campaign dress, elite company, 1812–13
The *9eme (bis) Hussards* existed from January 1812 until February 1813, when they became the 12th Hussars. Created from three squadrons of the 9th Hussars in Spain, their uniform was similar in the intervening period. This trumpeter's dolman would have been yellow with scarlet facings. By 1813 the trumpeters were newly equipped with white dolmans and pelisses, with light blue facings and scarlet lace, and light blue breeches ornamented with white lace. (Illustration after Knötel/Bucquoy)

G1 Captain of the 3rd Hussars in full dress, 1809–13
This extravagantly costumed officer would lead a company of two troops. This uniform would be strictly reserved for full dress occasions and a cheaper, simpler version employed in the field. Such was the enormous expense of these dress uniforms that the Bardin 1812 Regulations were established in order to restrict officially the huge sums sometimes required to kit out officers and heads of column in wasteful and impractical dress. When they came into force they were not totally successful, but they did prevent some of the wilder excesses of the early years being repeated when the Empire was still less able to afford it. (Illustration after Rousselot)

G2 Brigadier of the 12th Hussars in full dress, 1813–14
By this date overalls as shown here, being of rather better cut than their predecessors, were perfectly acceptable for full dress wear. Although they have buttons down the outer seams, these were by now redundant; the garment opened by means of a concealed button-up fly at the front. On first receipt of the *shakos rouleau*, hussars were inclined to append their old plumes to them, but this practice was soon quashed, leaving only the company-coloured pompon in its stead. A trooper of the elite company differed from this figure only in that his sleeves lacked the twin chevrons of corporals' rank,

and his *shako rouleau* was covered in scarlet cloth. (Illustration after Martinet/Carl Coll.)

G3 Trumpeter of the 1st Hussars in service dress, 1812
This trumpeter of a centre company contrasts considerably with those described in the captions to illustrations on pp. 30 and 31, which describe this regiment's trumpeters in 1814. It could be that those represented in black and white are dressed in uniforms issued under the First Restoration, but it is rather more likely that they simply belonged to different companies or squadrons; for, despite the express specifications of the 1812 Regulations, musicians' uniform persisted in being as varied as before, save that it was now intermingled with elements of the Imperial Livery, confusing the issue still further. (Illustration after Feist)

H1 Lieutenant of the 6th Hussars in service dress, 1814
This subaltern is clad in typical end-of-Empire style, the classic silhouette of the hussar uniform all but lost within the practical and civilian-influenced outline of the non-regulation cylindrical shako, slimmer-cut and shorter-than-ever pelisse, and trousers, these last reinforced with a double layer of fabric on the inner leg in place of the cumbersome inset leather. (Illustration after Rousselot)

H2 Maréchal-des-logis of the 4th Hussars in full dress, elite company, 1813–14
This sergeant is dressed and accoutred in the manner prescribed by the 1812 Regulations and it is immediately noticeable, and somewhat ironic, that the regulations devised to modernise and simplify the dress of the Imperial army appear a little to the right side of conservative in contrast to the up-to-the-minute fashions sported by the majority of hussars at this period. Purely for the sake of including it, we have employed a little licence in representing an NCO with the new *An IX/XIII*-pattern musketoon; in fact, neither NCOs or trumpeters were so armed, and nor, for that matter, was a large number of troopers. (Reconstruction)

H3 Trumpeter of the 2nd Hussars in full dress, 1812–14
In similar manner to the previous figure, this trumpeter is illustrated according to the 1812 Regulations, in this instance in the Imperial

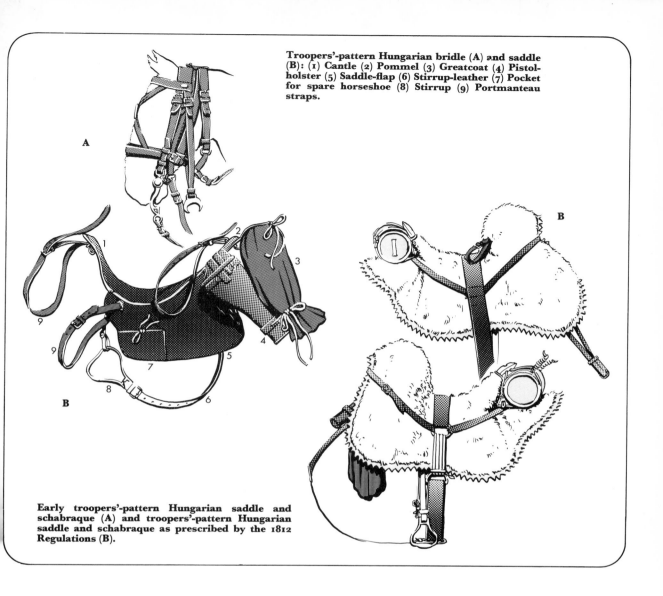

Troopers'-pattern Hungarian bridle (A) and saddle (B): (1) Cantle (2) Pommel (3) Greatcoat (4) Pistol-holster (5) Saddle-flap (6) Stirrup-leather (7) Pocket for spare horseshoe (8) Stirrup (9) Portmanteau straps.

Early troopers'-pattern Hungarian saddle and schabraque (A) and troopers'-pattern Hungarian saddle and schabraque as prescribed by the 1812 Regulations (B).

Livery. Designed to rationalise the dress of musicians throughout the Imperial army, it was only grudgingly accepted by the individual regiments, and often replaced with the regiment's own preferences within a very short time; consequently, it only added to the considerable diversity of musicians' uniforms. (Reconstruction after Bardin/Boisselier)

ERRATA
Colour figures A2, D3, F3, and G3 are illustrated wearing pelisses decorated with five vertical rows of buttons. Late information indicates that these figures should in fact be depicted with only three rows of buttons.

SOURCES

Anon., *Manoeuvres de la Cavalerie*

H. Bouchot, *L'Epopée du costume militaire française*

Cmndt. Bucquoy (Ed.), *Les Uniformes du 1er Empire*

French Ministry of War, *Historique des corps de troupe de l'armée française*

Dr Hourtouille (Ed.), *Soldats et uniformes du 1er Empire*

Job, *Tenue des troupes de France*

J. C. Quennevat, *Les vrais soldats de Napoléon*

Col. H. C. B. Rogers, *Napoleon's Army*

L. Rousselot, *L'armée française*

Various issues of the periodicals *La Giberne*, *Le Passepoil* and *La Gazette des Uniformes*.

Légendes des planches en couleurs

A1 Sous-lieutenant du 2eme Régiment en tenue de campagne, 1805. Bien qu'il ne manque aucun vêtement, tresse ou bouton à la représentation moderne du Hussard, il était rare de trouver des régiments ayant leur habillement et leur équipement au complet. **A2** Hussard du 2eme Régiment en grande tenue, 1801–2. Seuls les cordons et les raquettes de son bonnet à poil nous indiquent que cet individu n'est pas en tenue de route. **A3** Trompette du 4eme Régiment en grande tenue, 1804–5. Il porte le shako à flamme décrit par l'arrêté du 4 Brumaire An X qui, peu après sa consécration, n'était déjà plus au goût du jour.

B1 Lieutenant du 1er Régiment en tenue de service, 1805–7. Le bonnet de hussard, dépourvu de jugulaire avant 1805, était maintenu en place par un lacet en cuir, passant sous les cheveux liés en queue et fixé de chaque côté du fût. **B2** Hussard du 1er Régiment en tenue de campagne, 1806–8. **B3** Trompette du 5eme Régiment en grande tenue, 1805. Bien que le bleu ciel soit la couleur propre au 5eme Hussards, l'écarlate fut utilisé entre 1793 et 1802.

C1 Major du 8eme Régiment en tenue de service, vers 1809. Les majors de tous les corps de troupe de la Grande Armée portaient les mêmes insignes de grade que les colonels, mais se distinguaient par des galons de la couleur inverse. **C2** Hussard du 9eme Régiment en grande tenue, 1809. La ceinture écharpe, un écheveau de cordonnets long de 260cm, était garnie d'un noeud fixe à chaque extrémité. **C3** Trompette du 5eme Régiment en tenue de service, compagnie d'élite. D'après ses effets, nous pouvons constater qu'il date de l'époque 1808 à 1812.

D1 Lieutenant du 6eme Régiment en tenue de service, vers 1810. L'ouverture du petit pont de son pantalon de cheval nous indique que ce vêtement ressemble de plus en plus aux pantalons modernes. **D2** Brigadier-fourrier du 7eme Régiment en tenue de campagne, 1807–8. Le galon posé diagonalement sur son bras gauche est l'insigne du grade de fourrier. **D3** Trompette-major du 4eme Régiment en tenue de campagne, Espagne vers 1810. Les trompettes étaient indispensables à la transmission des signaux.

E1 Capitaine du 4eme Régiment en grande tenue, 1810. Il porte la tenue classique du hussard. **E2** Sapeur du 5eme Régiment en tenue de campagne, 1813. Remarquer la hauteur des manchettes en basane de son pantalon et l'insigne distinctif sur son sabretache. **E3** Trompette du 6eme Régiment en tenue de campagne, 1812. La fourrure blanche de son bonnet à poil et de sa pélisse, utilisée quotidiennement au début de l'Empire, s'avérait de plus en plus rare lors du crépuscule napoléonien.

F1 Chef d'escadron du 5eme Régiment en tenue de campagne, 1810–12. Créé en 1793, le grade de chef d'escadron était inférieur seulement à celui de chef de brigade. **F2** Sapeur du 1er Régiment en grande tenue, 1810–12. De la même manière que les sapeurs d'infanterie, les sapeurs de hussards composaient une garde autour du porte-aigle à la tête de la colonne. **F3** Trompette du 9eme (*bis*) Régiment en tenue de campagne, compagnie d'élite, 1812–13. Créé en janvier 1812, ce régiment devint le 12eme Régiment de Hussards en février 1813.

G1 Capitaine du 3eme Régiment en grande tenue, 1809–13. La tenue des officiers de hussards étant fort couteuse, le règlement de 1812, rédigé par le Major Bardin, avait pour intention la simplification de l'habillement afin de supprimer les vêtements et les accessoires superflus. **G2** Brigadier du 12eme Régiment en grande tenue, 1813–14. Un simple hussard de la compagnie d'élite aurait porté le même uniforme que ce sous-officier, mais avec le shako recouvert de drap rouge et avec l'exception des insignes de grade. **G3** Trompette du 1er Régiment en tenue de service, 1812. Bien que ce trompette ne ressemble pas à ceux du même régiment que nous avons inclus p. 30 et 31 il est vraisemblable qu'ils étaient de compagnies différentes.

H1 Lieutenant du 6eme Régiment en tenue de service, 1814. Nous constatons que la silhouette classique du hussard enfin cède le pas à l'influence de la mode contemporaine. **H2** Maréchal-des-logis du 4eme Régiment en grande tenue, 1813–14. Bien que les sous-officiers et les trompettes n'aient jamais été équipés de mousquetons, nous avons néanmoins fait figurer un mousqueton de l'An IX/XIII. **H3** Trompette du 2eme Régiment en grande tenue, 1812–14. Reconstitué d'après les détails fournis par le règlement de 1812, ce trompette porte la livrée impériale.

Farbtafeln

A1 Sous-Lieutenant der 2. Husaren im Feldzug, 1805. Obgleich sie mit vielen verschiedenen Uniformen ausgestattet waren, hatten die Husaren selten die volle Anzahl ihrer Ausrüstung. **A2** Reiter der 2. Husaren in Paradeanzug, 1801–2. Mit Ausnahme der Leinen und Troddel könnte diese Bild die Marschausrüstung darstellen. **A3** Trompeter der 4. Husaren in Paradeanzug, 1804–5. Der Tschako ist diesem späten Datum entsprechend untypisch, denn die *Flamme* gegen 1802 ausgefallen ist.

B1 Leutnant der 1. Husaren in Feldzug, 1805–7. Vor der Einführung von Sturmriemen in 1805, wurde die Kopfbedeckung durch einen Lederriemen, der unter dem Zopf des Trägers ührte, festgehalten. **B2** Reiter der 1. Husaren im Feldzug, 1806–8. **B3** Trompeter der 5. Husaren in Paradeanzug, 1805. Obgleich die 5. Husaren gewöhnlich himmelblaue Uniformen trugen, haben sie um 1793–1802 rote Rabatten getragen.

C1 Major der 8. Husaren im Feldzug, c. 1809. Majore von allen Gattungen der *Grande Armée* trugen dieselben Abzeichen als ihr Regimentsoberst, mit Tresse von der gegengesetzten Farbe als von dem Rest des Regiments getragen wurde. **C2** Reiter der 9. Husaren im Feldanzug, 1809. Die Leibbinde war 260cm lang mit festgemachten Kegeln an beiden Enden. **C3** Trompeter der 9. Husaren im Feldanzug, ausgewählte Kompagnie. Diese Figur stammt aus den Jahren 1808–12.

D1 Leutnant der 6. Husaren im Feldzug, c. 1810. Die engen Beinkleider, die mit einer Vorderlasche aufzumachen gingen, ähneln schon mehr gewöhnlichen Hosen. **D2** *Brigadier-fourrier* der 7. Husaren im Feldzug 1807–8. Der Rang *fourrier* wurde durch einen einfachen schrägen Streifen am linken Oberarm gezeigt. Dieser bestand aus Metalltresse von der selben Farbe als die Knöpfe. **D3** Stabstrompeter der 4. Husaren im Feldzug in Spanien c. 1810. Der Trompeter spielte die wichtige Rolle des Signalgebers.

E1 Hauptmann der 4. Husaren im Paradeanzug, 1810; die klassische Figur eines für Parade angezogenen Husars von hohem Dienstgrad. **E2** Pioneer der 5. Husaren im Feldanzug, 1813. Beachtenswert erscheint das Muster von gekreuzten Axten auf der Säbeltasche und die Aufschläge auf den Beinkleidern. **E3** Trompeter der 6. Husaren im Feldanzug, 1812. Obgleich in der früheren Kaiserzeit der weisse Fell der Bärenmütze und des Pelzes ziemlich üblich war, war er zu dieser Zeit als Luxus betrachtet.

F1 *Chef d'escadron* der 5. Husaren im Feldanzug 1810–12. Dieser Titel wurde im 1793 gegründet, und der *chef d'escadron* stand vom *chef de brigade* unmittelbar ab. **F2** Pioneer der 1. Husaren im Paradeanzug 1810–12. Dieser ausgewählte Reiter ritt mit dem Regimentsadler an der Spitze der Kolonne. **F3** Trompeter der 9. (bis) Husaren im Feldanzug, ausgewählte Kompagnie, 1812–13. Diese Einheit wurde in Januar 1812 aufgestellt, und wurde in Februar 1813 in die 12. Husaren umgewandelt.

G1 Hauptmann der 3. Husaren im Paradeanzug, 1809–13. Diese Paradeanzüge waren so ungeheuer kostbar, dass in 1812 die Bardin Verordnungen geschrieben worden sind, um die grössere Übertreibenheiten zu bändigen. **G2** *Brigadier* (Obergefreiter) der 12. Husaren im Paradeanzug, 1813–14. Ein Reiter der ausgewählten Kompagnie würde gleich aussehen, aber ohne den doppelten Tressenwinkel und mit einem mit scharlachrotem Tuch bezogenem Tschako. **G3** Trompeter der 1. Husaren im Feldanzug, 1812. Der Unterschied zwischen diesem Trompeter und denen an Seiten 30 und 31 dargestellten könnte daran liegen, dass sie zu verschiedenen Kompagnien gehörten.

H1 Leutnant der 6. Husaren im Feldanzug, 1814. Die klassische Husarensilhouette geht in die zivilbeeinflusste Linien der späten Kaiserzeit verloren. **H2** *Maréchal-des-Logis* der 4. Husaren im Paradeanzug 1813–14. Eine XI/XIII Flinte wird dargestellt, obgleich weder Unteroffiziere noch Trompeter hätten normalerweise solche Waffen getragen. **H3** Trompeter der 2. Husaren im Paradeanzug, kaiserliche Livree, 1812–14. Die Verordnungen von 1812 schrieben diese, zwar unbeliebte, kaiserliche Livree vor.